# KIDS' GUIDES

# JUDO

## by Thomas Buckley

Content Adviser: Philip S. Porter, Founder,
United States Martial Arts Association,
Citrus Heights, California

Published in the United States of America by The Child's World®
PO Box 326 • Chanhassen, MN 55317-0326 • 800-599-READ • www.childsworld.com

## ACKNOWLEDGMENTS

The Child's World®: Mary Berendes, Publishing Director

Editorial Directions, Inc.: E. Russell Primm, Editorial Director; Halley Gatenby, Line Editor;
Susan Hindman, Copyeditor; Elizabeth K. Martin and Katie Marsico, Assistant Editors;
Matthew Messbarger, Editorial Assistant; Kerry Reid, Fact Checker; Tim Griffin/IndexServ,
Indexer; James Buckley Jr., Photo Researcher and Photo Selector

The Design Lab: Kathleen Petelinsek, Design and Page Production

## PHOTOS

Cover: Reuters New Media/Corbis
TRBfoto/Photodisc, 1
AP/Wide World: 6, 20, 22
Bettmann/Corbis: 7
Duomo/Corbis: 8, 12
Getty Images: 13, 17
Jim Cummins/Corbis: 14, 24
Keerle Georges De/Corbis Sygma: 26
Langevin Jacques/Corbis Sygma: 10
Michael Maslan Historic Photographs/Corbis: 4
Michael S. Yamashita/Corbis: 28
Reuters NewMedia Inc./Corbis: 18, 19, 23, 25, 27
Tom & Dee Ann McCarthy/Corbis: 9

## LIBRARY OF CONGRESS CATALOGING-IN-PUBLICATION DATA

Buckley, Thomas J.
  Judo / by Thomas Buckley.
    p. cm. — (Kids' guides)
Contents: When the samurai put down their swords—Doctor Kano's fighting system—Learning
the art: training for balance—The judo arsenal: throwing and grappling—The gentle way—Judo is
for everyone.
  ISBN 1-59296-030-8 (Library Bound : alk. paper)
1. Judo—Juvenile literature. [1. Judo.] I. Title. II. Series.
GV1114.B78 2004
796.815'—dc22
                                                              2003018078

# CONTENTS

# PUTTING DOWN THE SWORD

## FOR CENTURIES, THE ISLAND NATION OF

Japan was ruled by a warrior class known as the samurai. The beginnings of judo can be found in the fighting practices of the samurai.

These men are dressed as samurai. Note the long swords, called *katana*.

All samurai were loyal to the emperor of Japan. Aside from that, though, the samurai were part of a feudal society. In this type of society, the land was broken up into different sections called provinces, each ruled by a lord known as a daimyo. These lords had their own armies of samurai warriors, and they often battled one another for territory.

This continual fighting made the samurai some of the mightiest warriors in history. They trained constantly with their famous swords, known as *katana.* They used **longbows** in their study of archery. They practiced fighting with spears and developed protective suits made of leather, metal, and bamboo. They also studied etiquette (courtly manners), special ceremonies, and calligraphy (fancy penmanship). But mostly they learned to fight.

Part of their training was what to do in case they ever lost their weapons. When that happened, they needed to be able to fight well with their bare hands. Many samurai were as dangerous unarmed as they were with their deadly swords.

The samurais' hand-to-hand combat training was based on jujitsu, an ancient form of fighting that is still practiced in Japan. Different jujitsu **masters** developed fighting techniques into an art. Each master created his own specific style, or *ryu.* Jujitsu is considered the origin of the sport known as judo.

# CHAPTER ONE

# DR. KANO'S FIGHTING SYSTEM

## THE FOUNDER AND CREATOR OF JUDO WAS

Jigoro Kano, a Japanese educator who hoped to preserve the spiritual, moral, and physical aspects of old jujitsu. Judo was not invented by a mighty warrior or a fierce wrestler. Dr. Kano was the principal of the University of Education in Tokyo, Japan. He was a small man, standing only 5 feet, 2 inches high. Even so, he developed one of the world's most popular and effective fighting systems.

Today, Dr. Kano's creation is one of the world's most popular fighting systems.

Dr. Kano began studying jujitsu at age 16 and became a master of jujitsu techniques. He studied under a number of masters. By his mid-20s, Dr. Kano had learned the most advanced and secret techniques of several of Japan's rival jujitsu ryu. As he studied, though, he found that the severe training methods and fierce attacks could sometimes result in injury to the participants.

It is important to remember that jujitsu was not developed for exercise or as a sport. It began as a way for soldiers in combat to protect themselves. The samurai practiced jujitsu

It didn't take long for Dr. Kano's new martial art to be practiced all over the world.

Judo is a safe and fun way for children to exercise their minds and bodies.

to survive on the battlefield. Because of this, jujitsu techniques can be very fierce, dangerous, and sometimes deadly! Dr. Kano wanted to transform jujitsu into more of a sport. He wanted a **martial art** that children could practice safely, to keep them physically active and more aware. To do this, he made several important changes to jujitsu. He eliminated the most dangerous techniques, such as gouging out eyes and breaking fingers.

One important element of the martial arts is to show respect for your opponent.

He also laid out a set of rules for participants to follow while sparring.

Two principles would govern this new sport. The first was *seiryoku zenyo*, meaning "maximum efficiency with minimum effort." The most important part of jujitsu was using an opponent's force against him or her. Dr. Kano kept this part in his new art because he believed it was the most efficient way to win. The second principle was *jita kyoei*, or "mutual benefit and welfare." Dr. Kano said that to follow this principle, players must have compassion and respect for their opponents.

In 1882, at a Buddhist temple in Tokyo, Dr. Kano introduced the art of judo, which is Japanese for "the gentle way." The throws and holds of jujitsu were still included. Judo,

Judo's best men and women compete in the Olympics every four years.

however, allowed students to practice with full force but without injury. The school he founded was called the Kodokan Judo Institute. *Kodokan* means "a place for learning the way." The Kodokan remains the international authority on judo.

Judo's popularity exploded in Japan when one of Dr. Kano's teams defeated a combined team from several well-known jujitsu ryu. Judo's popularity became international when one of Dr. Kano's students, Yoshiaki Yamashita, came to the United States. Yamashita taught judo to cadets at the U.S. Military Academy at West Point. He also taught President Theodore Roosevelt. Judo became even more popular after World War II, when U.S. military troops in Japan saw firsthand how effective judo could be.

Dr. Kano worked hard to get judo accepted as an Olympic sport, but he did not live to see his dream fulfilled. He died in 1938. The first Judo World Championships were held in 1956. Judo first entered the Olympics as a demonstration sport for men in 1964 and for women in 1988. It is now an official Olympic sport for both.

Dr. Kano's work was a success. He changed the deadly art of jujitsu into something more gentle and accessible. He created a powerful and popular martial art that is studied and practiced all over the world today.

# LEARNING THE ART

## TRAINING FOR JUDO HAS TWO MAIN PARTS.

A series of moves performed in a planned sequence is called a form, or **kata.** The kata helps students learn judo's throws, holds, and other techniques. The techniques are practiced over and over—with a partner or alone—until they can be done perfectly.

In judo—just like any other endeavor—practice makes perfect.

Sparring is an effective way for martial-arts students to develop their skills.

Sparring, or ***randori,*** takes place when the students face off against each other to practice their techniques. Because of the safety rules devised by Dr. Kano, these techniques can be performed without injury. Sparring practice allows students to learn their skills for self-defense or for tournament competition.

The most important thing for a ***judoka*** (a person who studies or practices judo) to learn is balance. This training begins with proper posture and stance. Before and during a

In all martial arts, maintaining proper balance is important, whatever the maneuver.

match, students stand in the **shizentai** (natural posture). They stand quietly, legs slightly bent, gripping their opponent's uniform with the hands. From this position, the judoka can move to meet or deliver any attack. He or she tries to remain firmly upright and balanced.

The shizentai also helps students remain loose so that they can keep that balance while moving quickly. This helps with flexibility, another important part of judo training.

Students stretch their muscles and joints before practice to remain flexible. Good stretching is important in any sport, but especially in judo. In fact, many judo throws and pins require great flexibility.

Judo students also train long and hard to develop strength and endurance. They do shoulder rolls and practice falls on the mat, which absorbs some of the impact. They build their leg muscles with special exercises. One of these is called the duck walk. To do this, students crouch down low, knees bent, and walk back and forth across the mat. It's not easy. Muscles can get sore.

Judo training usually takes place in a **dojo.** The students train on padded mats to avoid injury. They wear heavy, white cotton uniforms called judogi. Before a match begins, the competitors bow to each other very formally. It is always important in a judo match to show respect and courtesy for your opponent. Likewise, courtesy and respect are always paid to the referee and two judges who decide the winner of the match.

A judoka does not compete out of anger or hate, but only to practice and test his or her abilities. Judo is not about fighting with brute force but, rather, competing with skill, balance, grace, and courtesy. After the bow, the students face each other. Each grasps the other's sleeve and collar. They then try to throw each other. If they fall to the mat as a result of a throw, they **grapple** to pin each other or perform other techniques.

It is important in judo to practice with students of differing skill levels. A judoka develops skills and polishes techniques against a person at the same level of training. When the same judoka competes against a more advanced master, he or she can learn new techniques. When competing against someone with less experience, the judoka is both teacher and student. You learn more about your own techniques when you teach them to a younger student.

## UNIFORMS AND BELTS

You've probably seen martial artists in loose jackets and pants, almost like pajamas. They wear colored belts that tell you how advanced they are. The masters wear black belts.

Many martial arts, such as karate, kenpo, and tae kwon do, use uniforms similar to those worn in judo. Many also have a system of colored belts to show advances in learning or rank. Those uniforms and belts were first used in judo. Dr. Kano first had his advanced students wear black obi, or belts, with the **kimonos** they wore to practice. Beginner students wore white obi.

In 1907, Dr. Kano introduced judogi—white, strongly knit jackets and loose pants. They were similar to what students wear today. In 1935, the colored belts showing different ranks were introduced. The judogi were so comfortable and practical for martial arts training that many other arts soon adopted them. And the colored-belt ranking system worked so well that it was widely copied, too.

# THE JUDO ARSENAL

## DR. KANO WAS A SMALL MAN. HE WANTED

his sport to be one that anyone could do, whether that person had a small build like his or was larger and more powerful. He wanted judo to be enjoyed by children and grandparents and everyone in between. So he developed techniques that required balance and speed as well as strength. In fact, judo's secret lies in turning your opponents' strengths against them.

From the smallest to the biggest, every member of the family can enjoy judo.

One goal of judo is to put the attacker off balance. Imagine an opponent coming at you full force. If you are bigger or stronger, you can meet that force head on, like a football lineman. In that case, however, you take the full force of the attack. Dr. Kano realized that it is much better to maintain your balance and simply step aside. As the attacker rushes by, balance now lost, the judoka can throw that person to the ground.

Dr. Kano once fought a match against a famous wrestler, a huge man who claimed never to have been beaten. He must

An effective judoka uses an opponent's force to his or her advantage.

Sometimes, judo action is head over heels—or heels over head!

have been shocked when the wiry little doctor challenged him. But not as shocked as he was when Dr. Kano won the match! The wrestler couldn't get his hands on Dr. Kano. Every time he tried, the doctor glided gracefully out of reach and flung him to the ground. Finally, the wrestler gave up. He later became one of the doctor's students!

Judo is probably best known for its spectacular throws. Throwing techniques are called *nage-waza*. There are two types of throws: standing throws (*tachi-waza*) and sacrifice throws

A judo match often features spectacular throws such as this one.

*(sutemis-waza)*. Nage-waza techniques are performed from a standing position. The thrower *(tori)* keeps careful balance while flipping the opponent with the hands, hip, or leg. The one

being thrown is called the *uke*. Once the throw begins, the uke is off his feet and all balance is lost. All the strength and size in the world won't help if the tori has just flipped you over her hip and you're flying through the air.

While throws are better known, judo's *kateme-waza* (grappling or wrestling techniques) are also important. When two judoka meet, a throw or a counter can send them falling to the mat. They can continue to grapple on the mat. Most real-life encounters end with the combatants falling to the ground. For this reason, judo teaches a wide variety of grappling techniques that are important in self-defense.

*Osae-komi-waza* are hold-downs, or pinning techniques. The judoka learns different ways to control and pin an opponent with these holds.

*Kantsu-waza* are joint-locking techniques. Judoka use different holds to reverse the elbow joint of an opponent's arm in order to force him to surrender. Sometimes in randori training, a competitor's joint is reversed so strongly that he must give up.

*Shime-waza* are choking or strangling holds. The attacker uses the lapel of her opponent's judogi jacket against his neck to cut off air flow to the lungs or to reduce the blood going into the brain. These techniques can cause the opponent to lose consciousness.

Because kantsu-waza and shime-waza can cause injury, opponents are always given a chance to surrender. To do this, a student taps his attacker or the mat to let his opponent know he is surrendering. He is then released from the hold, and the other player is the winner.

Judo's striking techniques are called *atemi-waza*. Because of the danger of injury they pose, they are generally used only in kata or in real-life self-defense situations. Atemi-

Judoka must learn effective techniques when the action is down on the mat.

It can be a rough-and-tumble world in judo competition.

waza strikes can be made with the hands *(ude-ata)* or the feet *(ashi-ate)*. Because the techniques are so dangerous, advanced students can be taught to revive their opponents. These life-saving techniques are referred to as *kappo*. Even when its most dangerous moves are employed, judo still provides its masters with a way to help the opponent.

# CHAPTER FOUR

# THE GENTLE WAY

Dr. Kano believed that the goal of judo training is self-improvement. He once said:

> **The aim of Judo is to utilize physical and mental strength most effectively. Its training is to understand the true meaning of life through the mental and physical training of attack and defense. You must develop yourself as a person and become a useful citizen to society.**

The martial arts teach effective self-defense, as well as attack maneuvers.

Judo's aim is to help a person develop attitudes that are useful in a judo match and in everyday life. The first of these is the wa, which means "peace and harmony." The physical balance and giving-way of judo helps a person be balanced in mind as well. Judo masters have spent hours competing against other masters, so they are confident in their skill. Because of this, they have no desire or need to prove anything by fighting people of lesser skill. And when faced with a challenge, they do not need to resort to violence to prove how strong they are. They already know.

This attitude does not make a judoka brag or be arrogant. On the contrary, it allows the judoka to be very tolerant and accepting of other people. It also allows the judoka to live in peace with others, as Dr. Kano wanted.

If a fight becomes necessary for self-defense, judo teaches the lesson of *seiryoku zenyo*, or "maximum efficiency in energy."

Under the watchful eyes of the judges, two judo combatants grapple.

Judo is sometimes used to train military and police personnel such as the ones shown here.

With seiryoku zenyo, the judoka does only what is necessary to accomplish the task and does not waste energy. When attacked, the judo master does not meet the attack with equal force. Instead, the master does only what is needed to turn the attacker's force against him.

Perhaps most important to Dr. Kano, though, was the lesson of mutual benefit (*jita kyoei*). He called judo "training for life," and he felt that students should use it to develop self-discipline, respect, and courtesy for others. The ultimate aim of judo was—and is—to do everything possible to perfect a student so that he or she can be of value to society.

# JUDO IS FOR EVERYONE

## DR. KANO BEGAN HIS DEVELOPMENT OF

judo in part to avoid the injuries that could occur if students practiced jujitsu techniques while sparring. His hope was that judo could be used to teach self-discipline and respect to children and to improve their mental and physical health.

Because of this, the techniques of judo can be taught to anyone. Judo helps to strengthen and toughen a person's

International judo competitions can be intense and exciting.

Judo is taught in clubs and classes throughout the United States.

muscles. But great size or physical strength is not needed. Practicing and refining the techniques are far more important than size or strength.

Judo is taught all over the world, and its students range from small children to powerful Olympic athletes. There are judo clubs and teachers in just about every major city in the United States. Check your local phone book for dojos in your area, and visit them. You and your parents can decide which dojo is the right school for you.

While most students of judo are young, judo can also be taught to senior citizens. Your grandparents could learn the same techniques you do. Classes are also taught for the blind and for people with other special needs.

As Dr. Kano intended, anyone can use judo to help them lead a better life—and to fight "the gentle way."

# GLOSSARY

**dojo**—a school, or room, for practicing judo

**grapple**—to wrestle with another person using grabbing and holding techniques

**judoka**—a person who studies or practices judo

**kata**—a series of judo moves practiced in a planned sequence

**katana**—long, slightly curved, extremely sharp swords used by samurai

**kimonos**—long robes with wide sleeves worn outside of other clothing

**longbows**—wooden bows designed to be held vertically

**martial art**—a fighting sport or skill, especially one developed in Asia

**masters**—individuals especially skilled at an art or sport; their work serves as a model for others

**randori**—a type of judo practice that involves actual fighting and contact

**ryu**—a style of martial arts developed by a particular person or school

**shizentai**—the natural position, the first posture a judo student assumes to begin a match or a move

# TIMELINE

**1882** Dr. Kano founds the Kodokan Judo Institute in Tokyo and introduces judo.

**1886** At a tournament sponsored by the Tokyo Police Department, a team from the Kodokan Institute defeats a team of students from several jujitsu ryu.

**1904** Yoshiaki Yamashita goes to the United States to teach judo to cadets at the U.S. Military Academy at West Point and to President Theodore Roosevelt.

**1905** The association of black belt masters (Kodokan Yudanshakai) is founded, symbolizing judo's triumph over jujitsu in Japan.

**1918** Gunji Koizumi goes to England to found a judo school called the Budokwai.

**1940s** During World War II, U.S. soldiers serving in Asia see firsthand how effective judo can be. Many of them study judo and bring their training home to the United States after the war.

**1952** Sumiyuki Kotani trains the first U.S. Air Force Judo Team at the Kodokan Institute. General Curtis LeMay later requires judo for all Air Force Strategic Air Command combat crews.

**1956** The first Judo World Championships are held.

**1964** Judo becomes a demonstration Olympic sport for men in the Tokyo Olympics.

**1972** Men's judo becomes an official Olympic sport.

**1988** Judo becomes a demonstration Olympic sport for women in the Seoul Olympics.

**1992** Women's judo becomes an official Olympic sport.

# FIND OUT MORE

## Books

Bailey, Donna. *Judo*. Austin, Tex.: Steck-Vaughan, 1991.

Buckley, Thomas. *Karate*. Chanhassen, Minn.: The Child's World, 2004.

Collins, Paul. *Judo*. Broomall, Pa.: Chelsea House, 2001.

Horn, Douglas C. *Moves*. Unionville, N.Y.: Royal Fireworks Press, 1995.

Morris, Neil. *Judo*. Chicago: Heinemann Library, 2001.

## On the Web

Visit our home page for lots of links about judo:
*http://www.childsworld.com/links.html*

NOTE TO PARENTS, TEACHERS, AND LIBRARIANS: We routinely check our Web links to make sure they're safe, active sites—so encourage your readers to check them out!

# INDEX

# ABOUT THE AUTHOR

Thomas Buckley is an attorney and writer in Raleigh, North Carolina, who has won several screenwriting awards. In 1997, he was honored to earn a student black belt in Kenpo Karate from Grandmaster Rick Allemany in San Francisco. He has also participated in seminar training in the arts of jujitsu, *arnis, escrima, wing chun,* and kung fu Sansoo. His one-year-old son already has a pretty good front kick and an impressive *ki-ai,* and his five-year-old daughter is formidable!